THE NATURE KIDS GUIDE TO
CHAMELEONS

DAVID ANDERSON

LP Media Inc. Publishing
Text copyright © 2026 by LP Media Inc.
All rights reserved.

For information address LP Media Inc. Publishing,
30012 Variolite St NW, Princeton MN 55371
www.lpmedia.org

Publication Data

Chameleons
The Nature Kid's Guide to Chameleons — First edition.

Summary: "Learn all about Chameleons, the Nature Kid Way"
— Provided by publisher.

ISBN: 979-8-89818-154-3

[1. Chameleons – Non-Fiction] I. Title.

Title: The Nature Kid's Guide to Chameleons

CONTENTS

TREETOP HOMES
4

Rustle! A chameleon grips a branch. Its tail curls tight.

Most chameleons live high up in trees. Their feet grip branches like clamps. Each foot has toes that work like pincers, which helps them hold on tight.

Chameleons live in warm places. They need heat from the sun, so forests and jungles are perfect homes. Some also live in dry scrublands.

Trees give chameleons what they need. Leaves hide them from danger. Branches let them hunt for bugs. The treetops are home for many chameleons.

A chameleon's tail can wrap around branches like a fifth hand. This helps them balance as they climb.

HOME RANGE

Click! A chameleon climbs a tree in Africa. It grips the branch tight.

Most chameleons live in Africa. About half of all **species** live on the island of Madagascar.

But some chameleons live in other places too. A few species live in southern Europe. Others live in parts of Asia.

Some chameleons have escaped from pet owners in places like Hawaii and Florida. These chameleons don't belong there. They can harm the native animals.

The veiled chameleon lives high in the mountains where winters can drop to freezing!

TINY TO TALL

Snap! A tiny chameleon sits on a thumb. It is smaller than a grape!

Chameleons come in many sizes. A young Brookesia micra can fit on the tip of a match! This tiny lizard is only about one inch long.

The Parson's chameleon is one of the biggest. It can grow over two feet long. That is about as long as a house cat!

Most chameleons are somewhere in between. Many are about the size of a pencil.

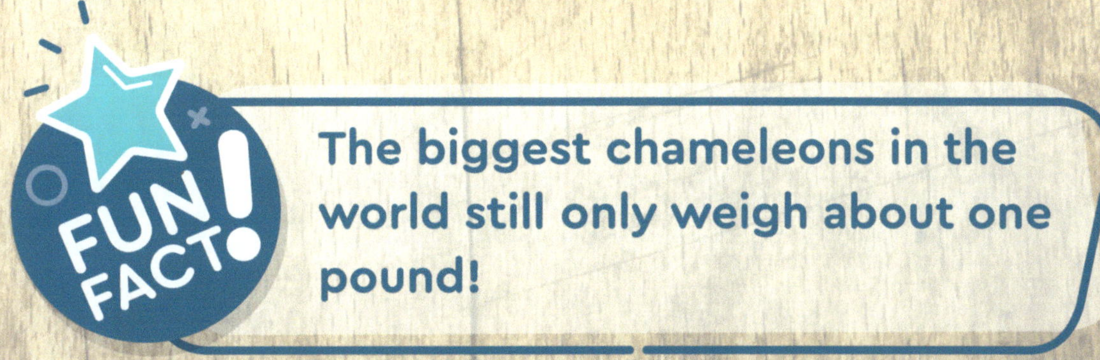

The biggest chameleons in the world still only weigh about one pound!

COOL BODIES

DID YOU KNOW?

A chameleon's tongue has a sticky tip. It can grab bugs faster than you can blink!

Whoosh! A chameleon swivels its eyes. Each eye moves alone.

Chameleons have amazing bodies. Their eyes can move in two directions at once. One eye can look forward while the other looks back!

Their tails are special too. A chameleon's tail can wrap around branches. It works like an extra hand. The tail helps them balance as they climb.

Chameleons have bumpy skin. Some have horns or crests on their heads. These bumps and shapes help them blend in with bark and leaves.

SUPER
SIGHT

Swivel! A chameleon looks two ways at once. Amazing!

Chameleons have super eyes. They can see almost all around them without moving their heads.

Each eye works on its own. One eye can look up while the other looks down. This helps them spot bugs and danger at the same time.

Chameleons can also see colors that humans cannot see!

A chameleon can spot a tiny bug from 30 feet away! That is as long as a school bus!

COLOR CHANGERS

Flash! A chameleon's skin shifts from brown to green.

Chameleons are famous for changing color. But they do not change to match their surroundings. They change color based on mood and temperature.

A calm chameleon may look pale green. An angry one may turn dark or show bright spots. Colors also change when a chameleon gets too hot or cold.

Special cells in their skin make this happen. These cells hold bits of color.

Chameleons can change color in about 20 seconds. That is super fast!

BUG
BUFFET

Flick! A chameleon catches a cricket. Lunch is served!

Chameleons eat many kinds of insects. They love crickets, grasshoppers, and flies. Some also munch on beetles and moths.

Bigger chameleons eat bigger meals. Large species may eat small lizards or baby birds. But most chameleons stick to insects.

Chameleons do not drink from puddles. Instead, they lick water drops off leaves. They often drink morning dew this way.

A young chameleon may eat up to 50 insects each day!

TONGUE ZAP

A chameleon's tongue goes from zero to 60 mph in one-hundredth of a second!

Thump! A sticky tongue hits a fly. Got it! The hunt is over in a flash.

Chameleons have amazing tongues. Their tongues can be longer than their whole bodies! They use them to catch food.

A chameleon's tongue shoots out super fast. It can hit a bug in less than one second. The tip is sticky and shaped like a cup, which helps grab prey.

The tongue works like a rubber band. Muscles squeeze it tight, then it snaps forward with great power. The tongue speeds up faster than a jet plane!

Once the tongue grabs a bug, it pulls back quickly. Don't blink or you'll miss it!

WATCH OUT

Hiss! A snake slithers closer. The chameleon stays very still.

Chameleons face many dangers in the wild. Snakes are their biggest threat. Tree snakes hunt them in branches.

Birds also eat chameleons. Hawks snatch them from trees.

Some mammals hunt chameleons too. Monkeys grab them while climbing.

With so many predators, baby chameleons face the most danger. They are small and easy to catch.

HIDE AWAY

Crunch! Leaves shake nearby. A chameleon freezes like a statue.

Chameleons have clever ways to hide. When danger comes, they stay perfectly still. This makes them hard to spot among leaves.

Many chameleons flatten their bodies. They press against branches to look like bark. Their bumpy skin helps them blend in.

Some drop to the ground and play dead. Others hide behind leaves. Staying hidden keeps them safe.

When a chameleon plays dead, it can stay frozen for up to 30 minutes until danger passes!

SLOW STROLL

Stomp! A chameleon takes one slow step. Then another.

Chameleons are very slow movers. They walk with a rocking motion. This helps them look like leaves swaying in the wind.

Their feet grip branches tightly. Each foot has toes that work like mittens.

Moving slowly helps chameleons stay hidden. Quick movements catch a predator's eye. A slow stroll keeps them safe.

Some chameleons take 10 minutes to move just 10 feet. That's slower than a snail!

DAY DWELLERS

Chirp! The sun rises. A chameleon wakes up and starts to move.

Chameleons are active during the day. This means they are **diurnal** animals. Sunlight warms their bodies and gives them energy.

Mornings are busy times. Chameleons bask in the sun first. Then they hunt for food.

At night, chameleons sleep on branches. They turn pale colors while resting. Even asleep, their grip stays strong on the branch.

Chameleons sleep about 12 hours each night. They often pick the same sleeping spot every evening.

LONER LIFE

Snarl! A chameleon puffs up. Another one came too close!

Chameleons like to live alone. They do not form groups or herds. Each chameleon stays in its own space.

Males can be very **territorial**. They puff up and show bright colors to scare others away. If one does not leave, fights can happen.

Chameleons only come near each other to mate.

Baby chameleons are on their own from the moment they hatch! They know how to hunt right away.

FLASHY
FLIRTS
30

Buzz! A male chameleon turns bright orange. He wants to be seen!

Male chameleons put on colorful shows. They flash bright yellows, reds, and blues. These bold colors help them stand out.

Females watch the displays. A female may show dark colors with spots. This means she is not interested.

If a female stays calm and shows light colors, mating may happen. After mating, both chameleons go their separate ways.

A female chameleon can remember a male's colors for days and know if she likes him!

CUTE CLUTCHES

Crack! A tiny egg breaks open. A baby chameleon peeks out.

Most chameleons lay eggs. A female digs a hole in soft dirt. She lays her eggs inside and covers them up.

A group of eggs is called a **clutch**. Some clutches have just 2 eggs. Others can have up to 200 eggs! The eggs stay buried for many months.

Baby chameleons hatch fully formed. They are tiny but look like adults. They can even hunt bugs right away! No parent helps them, so they must survive on their own.

ON THEIR OWN

Squeak! A young chameleon walks alone. No parent is there to help.

Baby chameleons never meet their parents. The mother leaves after laying her eggs and does not come back.

When babies hatch, they must find food alone. They climb trees by themselves, with no one to teach them how to hunt or hide.

Young chameleons know what to do by **instinct**. Their brains tell them how to catch bugs and to stay still when danger is near. Each baby takes care of itself from day one.

Newborn chameleons are jellybean-sized but catch bugs in minutes!

MAGIC
MOVES
36

Sway! A chameleon rocks back and forth, swaying like a leaf in the breeze.

Chameleons have a special walk. They rock their bodies side to side. This makes them look like leaves blowing in the wind.

Their tails can grip branches like an extra hand. They wrap around twigs and hold on tight.

Chameleons can also puff up their bodies. This makes them look bigger to scare enemies away.

Chameleons have feet split into two toe groups that work like mittens, giving them a super strong grip!

CARE TIPS

A pet chameleon climbs its branch. Time for a mist spray!

Chameleons need special care as pets. They need a tall cage with lots of branches to climb.

They must have warm lights and cool spots. A heat lamp helps them stay healthy. They also need misting so they can drink water drops.

For food, chameleons eat live bugs like crickets, roaches, and worms. They need careful owners who can give them just the right care!

Chameleons do not like to be held. Too much touching can make them feel stressed.

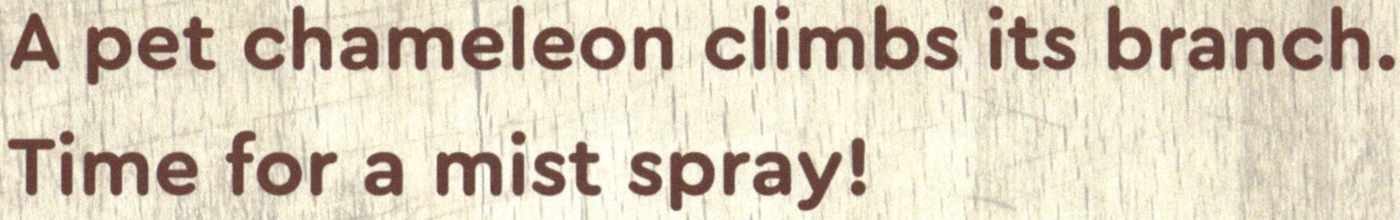

GLOSSARY

diurnal

An animal that is awake during the day and sleeps at night.

species

A group of animals that are the same kind.

territorial

When an animal protects its own space and doesn't want others nearby.

clutch

A group of eggs laid together by a mother animal.

instinct

Something an animal knows how to do without being taught.